11/25/2019

SCARY STATES
(OF MIND)

HORROR IN
ILLINOIS

by Alex Giannini

Consultant: Debbie Felton
Professor of Classics
University of Massachusetts
Amherst, Massachusetts

BEARPORT
PUBLISHING

New York, New York

Credits

Cover, © Mark Baldwin/Shutterstock and © Dudarev Mikhail/Shutterstock; TOC, © Danita Delmont/
Shutterstock; 4–5, © Mark Baldwin/Shutterstock, © Budimir Jevtic/Shutterstock, and © fizkes/
Shutterstock; 6, © Nadia Vella/CC BY-SA; 7, © Rick Drew; 8, Public Domain; 9, © faestock/Shutterstock
and © REDPIXEL.PL/Shutterstock; 10, © Mike_shots/Shutterstock; 11, © 3quarks/Shutterstock and The
Paranormal Guide/CC BY-SA 4.0; 12, © pran/Shutterstock; 13, Joe Therasakdhi/Shutterstock; 14, © Elihu
Vedder/Public Domain; 15L, Public Domain; 15R, © Katz PaganStar; 16, Public Domain; 17, Public
Domain; 18, © Ryan Davis/The Midwest Hiker; 19, © Chronicle/Alamy; 20, © Christin Lola/Shutterstock;
21, © KathySG/Shutterstock and Public Domain; 23, © Eddie J. Rodriguez/Shutterstock; 24, © PiXXart/
Shutterstock.

Publisher: Kenn Goin
Senior Editor: Joyce Tavolacci
Creative Director: Spencer Brinker
Photo Researcher: Thomas Persano
Cover: Kim Jones

Library of Congress Cataloging-in-Publication Data

Names: Giannini, Alex, author.
Title: Horror in Illinois / by Alex Giannini.
Description: New York : Bearport Publishing Company, Inc., 2020. l Series:
  Scary states (of mind) l Includes bibliographical references and index.
Identifiers: LCCN 2019007185 (print) l LCCN 2019017813 (ebook) l ISBN
  9781642805697 (Ebook) l ISBN 9781642805154 (library)
Subjects: LCSH: Haunted places—Illinois—Juvenile literature. l
  Ghosts—Illinois—Juvenile literature. l Illinois—Miscellanea—Juvenile
  literature.
Classification: LCC BF1472.U6 (ebook) l LCC BF1472.U6 G5253 2020 (print) l
  DDC 133.109773—dc23
LC record available at https://lccn.loc.gov/2019007185

For more information, write to Bearport Publishing Company, Inc., 45 West 21st Street,
Suite 3B, New York, New York 10010. Printed in the United States of America.

10 9 8 7 6 5 4 3 2 1

Contents

HORROR IN ILLINOIS

Illinois is known for its icy winters. However, there are things in the state far more alarming than the cold. Moans echo in the woods. Restless **spirits** haunt the living. A **mysterious** beast is on the loose.

Get ready to read four
spooky stories about Illinois.
Turn the page . . . if you dare.

RESURRECTION MARY

Resurrection Cemetery, Justice

This **cemetery** near Chicago is one of Illinois's most haunted places. It's the home of **Resurrection** Mary. This famous spirit has taken people on a wild, spooky ride.

The entrance to Resurrection Cemetery

6

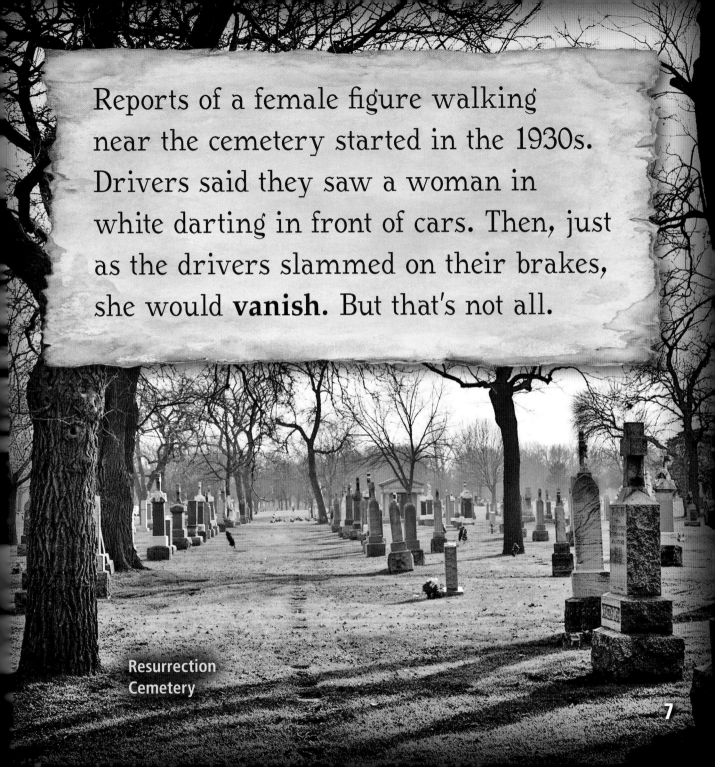

Reports of a female figure walking near the cemetery started in the 1930s. Drivers said they saw a woman in white darting in front of cars. Then, just as the drivers slammed on their brakes, she would **vanish.** But that's not all.

Resurrection Cemetery

In 1939, Chicago **resident** Jerry Palus met a woman in a white dress at a dance. When they held hands, she was ice cold. Later, Jerry drove her home. At Resurrection Cemetery, the woman said, "This is where I have to get out." The woman opened the car door and walked toward the graveyard. Just before she reached it, she disappeared!

Jerry Palus

Many people believe Resurrection Mary is the ghost of a young woman. **Legend** says she was on her way home from a dance when she was hit by a car and died.

9

THE ENFIELD HORROR

The McDaniel House, Enfield

In April 1973, Henry McDaniel heard scratching at his door. He opened it and saw a creature with two red eyes as big as flashlights! The monster had three legs and grayish skin. Henry couldn't believe his eyes.

11

Henry grabbed his gun and fired at the beast. He said it "hissed like a wildcat" and ran off.

When the police arrived, the creature was gone. However, they found scratch marks on the door and three strange footprints in the yard.

The three-legged creature was never caught. To this day, it's known as the Enfield Horror.

On May 6, 1973, Henry saw the monster again in the middle of the night.

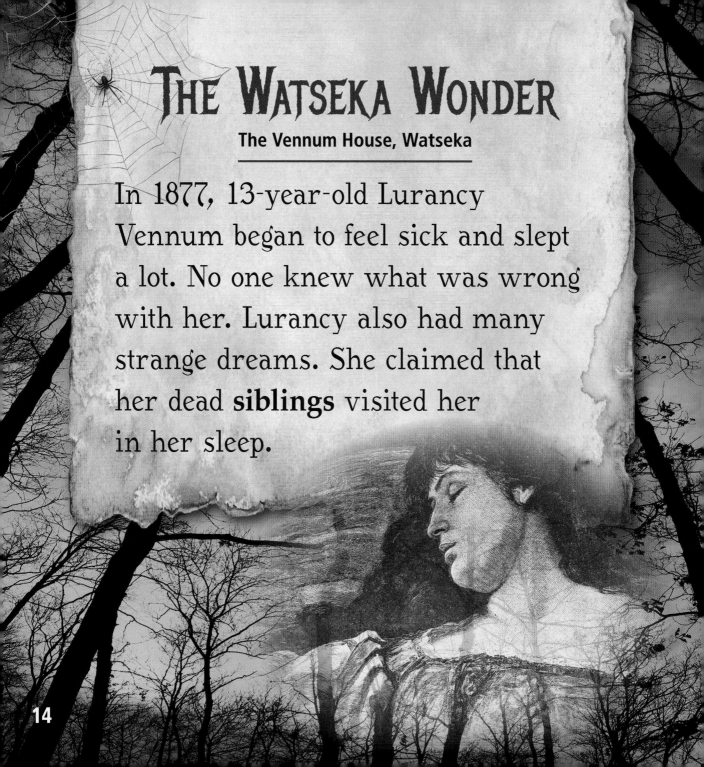

THE WATSEKA WONDER

The Vennum House, Watseka

In 1877, 13-year-old Lurancy
Vennum began to feel sick and slept
a lot. No one knew what was wrong
with her. Lurancy also had many
strange dreams. She claimed that
her dead **siblings** visited her
in her sleep.

Lurancy also said that spirits followed her. Her parents were troubled. What was wrong with their daughter?

The Vennum House today

An old photo of the Vennum House

Asa Roff, a local man, didn't believe Lurancy was ill. He thought she could speak with spirits of the dead! Through Lurancy, Asa contacted his dead daughter, Mary. Then, Mary **possessed** Lurancy's body. Amazingly, Lurancy knew things that only Mary and her family could know.

Lurancy's family grew worried. Mary's spirit didn't want to leave. After some time, however, Mary was driven from Lurancy's body for good.

Lurancy Vennum   Mary Roff

Eventually, Lurancy Vennum (far left in chair) married and raised her own family.

Lurancy Vennum became known as The Watseka Wonder.

17

A Ghost in the Devil's Oven

Devil's Backbone Park, Grand Tower

Near the Mississippi River in Illinois are rocks that stick out like a human **spine.** The rocks are known as the Devil's Backbone. Near the rocks is a hole that looks like a big oven. From this spot, called the Devil's Bake Oven, visitors sometimes hear an **eerie** moaning. Is the hole home to a lonely ghost?

The Devil's Backbone and surrounding parkland

An illustration of the
Mississippi River near
the Devil's Bake Oven

In the 1850s, a young woman named Esmerelda fell in love with a Mississippi riverboat captain. When her father **forbade** her from seeing him, Esmerelda locked herself in her room.

One day, she learned that the captain had drowned. Heartbroken, Esmerelda threw herself off the Devil's Bake Oven. She crashed into the river below.

Today, wailing can be heard near the rocky hole. Visitors have even seen a cloud of mist in the shape of a woman. Is it Esmerelda's ghost?

Spooky Spots in Illinois

WISCONSIN

Lake Michigan

THE VENNUM HOUSE
See where spirits possessed a young girl.

RESURRECTION CEMETERY
Does a troubled spirit haunt this cemetery?

IOWA

INDIANA

ILLINOIS

THE MCDANIEL HOUSE
Meet a terrifying creature with red eyes and three legs.

MISSOURI

CANADA

KENTUCKY

UNITED STATES

MEXICO

DEVIL'S BACKBONE PARK
Hear the wailing of a lonely ghost, looking for her lost love.

GLOSSARY

cemetery (SEM-uh-ter-ee) an area of land where dead bodies are buried

eerie (IHR-ee) strange and frightening

forbade (fer-BAYD) ordered not to

legend (LEJ-uhnd) a story from the past that is often not entirely true

mysterious (miss-TIHR-ee-uhss) very hard to explain or understand

possessed (puh-ZEST) to be controlled by something, such as a spirit

resident (REZ-uh-dent) a person who lives in a particular place

resurrection (rez-uh-REK-shun) a return to life after death

siblings (SIB-lings) brothers or sisters

spine (SPINE) the part of the skeleton that runs from the skull to the lower back

spirits (SPIHR-its) supernatural beings, such as ghosts

vanish (VAN-ish) to disappear

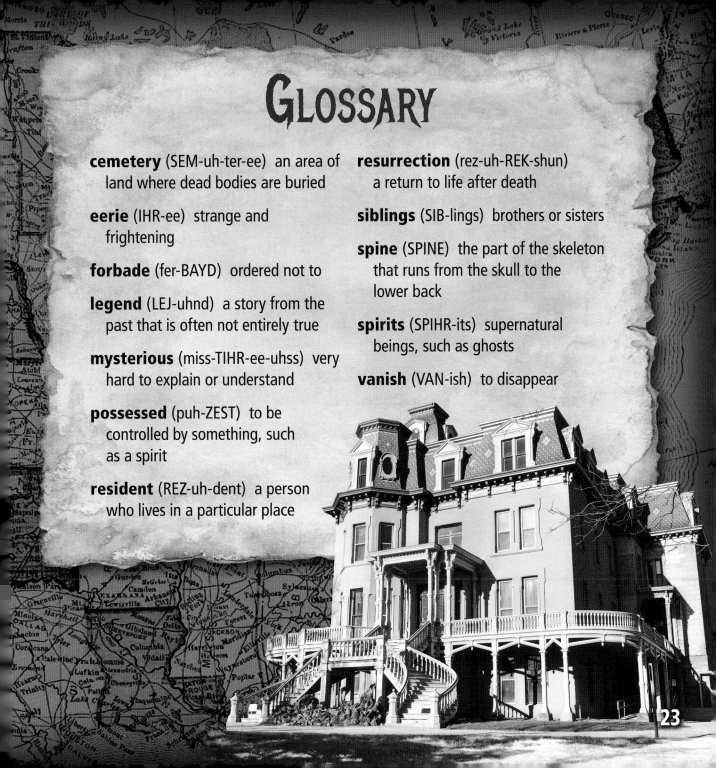

23

Index

Read More

Goddu, Krystyna Poray. *Creepy Chicago (Tiptoe Into Scary Cities).* New York: Bearport (2019).

Markovics, Joyce. *Chilling Cemeteries (Tiptoe Into Scary Places).* New York: Bearport (2017).

Learn More Online

To learn more about the horror in Illinois, visit:

www.bearportpublishing.com/ScaryStates

About the Author

Alex Giannini is a writer who also works in a public library. In his free time, he likes to hunt for ghost stories.